PIONEERS OF SCIENCE

ALBERT EINSTEIN

Peter Lafferty

The Bookwright Press
New York · 1992

Pioneers of Science

Archimedes
Alexander Graham Bell
Karl Benz
Marie Curie
Thomas Edison
Albert Einstein

Michael Faraday
Galileo
Guglielmo Marconi
Isaac Newton
Louis Pasteur
Leonardo da Vinci

First published in the
United States in 1992 by
The Bookwright Press
387 Park Avenue South
New York, NY 10016

First published in 1991 by
Wayland (Publishers) Ltd
61 Western Road, Hove
East Sussex BN3 1JD, England

© Copyright 1991 Wayland (Publishers) Limited

Library of Congress Cataloging-in-Publication Data
Lafferty, Peter.
    Albert Einstein / by Peter Lafferty.
        p. cm.—(Pioneers of science)
    Includes bibliographical references and index.
    Summary: Describes the life and work of the scientist whose theory
of relativity revolutionized scientific thinking.
        ISBN 0–531–18458–7
        1. Einstein, Albert, 1879–1955–Juvenile literature.
2. Physicists–Biography–Juvenile literature. [1. Einstein,
Albert, 1879–1955. 2. Physicists.]
        I. Title.   II. Series.
QC16.E5L24   1992
530'.092–dc20
[B]   91–15774
                                                                        CIP
                                                                        AC

Typeset by DP Press Ltd, Sevenoaks, Kent
Printed in Italy by Rotolito Lombardo S.p.A.

Contents

The Speedy Miss Bright

There once was a lady called Bright,
Who could travel faster than light;
She went out one day,
In a relative way,
And came back the previous night.

This limerick is not really about a woman called Miss Bright. It is really about a scientist called Albert Einstein, who was the greatest scientist of this century. In 1905, he put forward ideas that were so revolutionary that most people, even scientists, could not believe or understand them.

Once, when Einstein was visiting Hollywood, California, he rode down the street in a car with Charlie Chaplin, the famous movie actor. On the sidewalks, the excited crowd cheered and clapped the two famous men. Chaplin turned to his friend and said, "The people are applauding you because none of them understands you, and applauding me because everyone understands me."

But the limerick does tell us something about Einstein's ideas concerning what happens when objects move at very high speeds. Miss Bright is said to have traveled faster than light. That is very fast indeed. The speed of light is about 186,000 miles (300,000 kms) per second – 10,000 times faster than the fastest rocket. At this speed, you could travel around the world seven times in one second.

Einstein discovered that when objects approach the speed of light, strange effects occur. If clocks traveled at nearly the speed of light, they would appear to be slow or, to put it another way, time

Einstein had a great sense of fun. Here he shows that even great men should not be taken too seriously.

would slow down. According to Einstein, time travel into the future is possible (but not into the past as Miss Bright is said to have achieved). To Einstein, common sense was not a good guide to what happens at high speed.

Einstein did not do experiments to make his discoveries, as many scientists do. He was a "theoretical" scientist, who was concerned with "theories," or sets of ideas used to explain how nature works. He used mathematics to explore and explain the world and liked to do "thought experiments," in which he imagined doing something unusual. Then he would ask himself, "Is that possible? What would happen next?"

One of Einstein's thought experiments concerned a person looking into a mirror while illuminated by a lamp. If the mirror and the person were to suddenly shoot off at the speed of light, leaving the lamp behind, what would happen? Common sense says that the light from the lamp would never catch up with the mirror; therefore, at this speed, the person would no longer see his or her reflection in the mirror. But Einstein thought that this could not really happen. It must be impossible, Einstein decided, to travel as fast as light. So, alas, Miss Bright could not travel faster than, or even as fast as, light.

Einstein learned to play the violin when he was young. He was a good musician and gave public concerts to raise money for worthy causes.

Einstein sets out for a walk. Sometimes he became so engrossed in his thoughts about scientific problems that he lost his way and had to telephone a friend to get directions home.

Here is a thought experiment. Imagine that you are on a spaceship in outer space. Another spaceship approaches from the opposite direction at nearly the speed of light. According to Einstein, if we could see a clock on the approaching spaceship it would seem to be running slow. Can you imagine the situation from the point of view of the people on the other spaceship? To them, your spaceship would seem to be approaching them at great speed. So, according to Einstein, they would think that your clock was running slow. Who is correct? Whose clock is *really* running slow? Einstein's answer to this question is that it is impossible to decide which clock is "correct," so both groups of people have equal right to think their clock is correct.

Einstein discusses his work with an astronomer at the Mount Wilson Observatory, California. Proof that his ideas were correct came from observing the stars and planets.

How can scientists make any predictions about the future if they cannot be sure what the correct time is? Einstein saw that what was needed was a new theory, one that was correct no matter how things were moving. After years of thought, Einstein put forward a theory – called the theory of special relativity – which could be used to describe what happens at very high speeds.

The new theory opened up a whole new world of unexpected wonders. It shows not only that clocks slow down at high speeds but also that solid objects shrink at these speeds. A spaceship that was 330 ft (100 m) long when it took off, would appear to be only 280 ft (85 m) long if it passed your ship at half the speed of light.

Albert Einstein was born on March 14, 1879, in the small town of Ulm in southern Germany. Albert's father, Hermann, was an electrical engineer who had a small factory in the town. He was not a successful businessman, and his business failed before Albert was a year old. The Einstein family then moved to the German town of Munich to make a fresh start.

Albert with his younger sister Maja. Albert was a quiet child and was close to his sister. They remained good friends all their lives.

9

Einstein's mother, Pauline. She never doubted that her son was special, even when his teacher said, "He will never make a success of anything."

Although the Einstein family was Jewish, they did not follow many of the usual Jewish customs. Hermann thought that such things as going to the Jewish temple to worship and not eating pork were merely ancient superstitions. Indeed, at the age of five, Albert was sent to a Catholic elementary school.

Einstein's mother, Pauline, liked music, and she encouraged Albert to learn the violin at the age of six. Throughout his life Albert retained his love of music and he became an accomplished player of the violin.

Albert appears to have been slow to learn, and some of his teachers considered him a little backward. He was nine years old before he could speak fluently, and he appears to have been a quiet child, as his nurse nicknamed him "Father Bore." But, nevertheless, his mother was often heard to say to Albert that he would one day become a great professor.

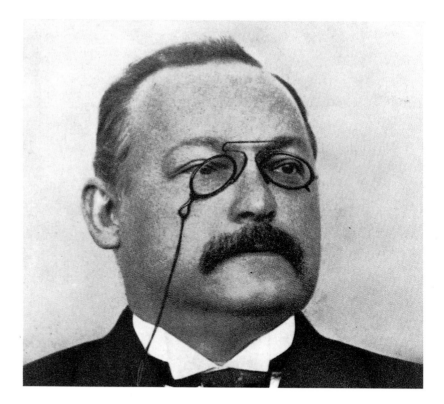

Einstein's father, Hermann. He was an electrical engineer and an unsuccessful businessman. He started with a factory in Munich, Germany, and then moved the family to Milan, Italy, in search of success.

When Albert was five years old, his father showed him a pocket compass. Young Albert was fascinated by the invisible force that turned the needle northward. It was his first encounter with a "force field," a region in which the effects of a force can be seen. Later he was to develop theories to explain how some force fields work.

Albert was also intrigued by his Uncle Jakob's description of algebra: "We go hunting for a little animal whose name we don't know, so we call it '*x*.' When we bag our game we pounce on it and give it its right name." To his uncle, algebra was a "merry science."

At the age of ten, Albert entered secondary school. He was not a good pupil, and he disliked the school's strict, almost military, discipline. He did, however, make a great effort at mathematics. He liked to study geometry, in particular; being able to discover things about the world by pure thought thrilled him.

Einstein (seated first on the left) with his classmates at the school in Aarau, near Zurich, in 1896. He spent a year studying there for his Polytechnic entrance examination, which he had failed at the first attempt.

He also began to read books about science. The books were lent to him by a student who visited his family each week. The two became friends and had long conversations about science and mathematics.

When Albert was fifteen, his mother, father and younger sister, Maja, moved to Milan in Italy. Albert was left behind to complete his studies, but within six months he was expelled from school for being disruptive, so Albert followed his family to Italy.

Although Albert liked Italy, with its sense of freedom and history, he did not stay with his family for long. About a year later, he moved to the Swiss city of Zurich to try to enter the Swiss Polytechnic, which could be attended by anyone who passed the entrance examination – even someone like Albert who did not have a school certificate. At sixteen, he would have been its youngest pupil but, unfortunately, he did not pass the examination.

For the next year, he studied at a school near Zurich. He enjoyed life in Switzerland – Swiss schooling was completely different from that in Germany. The people were tolerant, and the mountain scenery was breathtaking. He decided to renounce his German citizenship, and for a while he was officially without a nationality.

At the age of seventeen, he passed the polytechnic entrance examination and started studying for a teacher's degree with the idea of teaching physics and mathematics. But he found the lectures boring and did not always attend. His friend, Marcel Grossmann, took meticulous notes at the lectures, which he gladly let Albert study. Albert preferred to learn by reading the works of famous scientists. In this way, he learned about the new questions science was trying to answer.

In 1900, he completed his studies and the following year was granted Swiss citizenship. Finding a permanent job proved difficult, and for about a year he did little. Then, in 1902, he became a low-grade clerk at the Swiss Patent Office in the city of Bern. His job was to examine the models and plans sent in by hopeful inventors.

Albert Einstein with his first wife, Mileva. She was a mathematician and helped Einstein with his work. In 1900, Albert wrote to Mileva, "How happy and proud I will be when the two of us together will have brought our work on the relative motion to a victorious conclusion."

He had to see how the inventions worked and then write a description of them, to establish the inventor's legal ownership of the idea. He called his work at the Patent Office his "shoemaker's job." This did not mean that he regarded the work with contempt. On the contrary, he enjoyed the work and it gave him time for his study and research. Realizing the advantages of an undemanding job, he said, "Every scientist should have a shoemaker's job."

In 1903, he married a young woman he had known from his student days, a mathematician named Mileva Maric. At this time, Albert was beginning to publish his ideas in scientific magazines, or journals. Although his work was still largely unknown, he was on the verge of one of this century's most astounding discoveries.

A portrait of Einstein painted about the time of his great discoveries.

High-Speed Science

In 1905, Einstein published details of his revolutionary theory of special. relativity – the theory that deals with the effects of high-speed motion.

Einstein realized that at very high speeds – near the speed of light – commonsense ideas break down. Imagine, for example, that you are driving a car along a road at a speed of 60 mph (as shown on the speedometer). Another car approaches from the opposite direction, also traveling at 60 mph (as shown on its speedometer). To you, the other car will appear to be approaching at a speed of 120 mph. In this situation, your common sense tells you that the speeds of the two cars are added together.

Now replace the approaching car with a beam of light. If your car is still, the light beam approaches

Einstein (right) with two friends, Howard Habult and Maurice Solovine. They formed a debating society called the "Academy" to discuss the latest scientific research, which helped Einstein to work out his ideas.

The effects of high speed

Imagine that an astronaut has left earth traveling at 90 percent of the speed of light. The astronaut would not notice anything strange, but to us, left on earth, the effects of the high speed would be very noticeable. The mass of the spacecraft would double, and it would be less than half its original length. A clock on board would take an hour to record 26 minutes because time would have slowed. The astronaut would age at half the rate of a twin left behind on earth. When the astronaut returned to earth, the twin left on earth would be twice as old as the space traveler.

you at a speed of 186,000 miles per second. If you speed toward the approaching light at 60 miles per second, you would expect the beam to approach you at 186,060 miles per second. But it does not! The light actually approaches you at 186,000 miles per second. In fact, as Einstein realized, whatever speed you travel at, the light always approaches at exactly the same speed. If you speed away from the beam, the same thing happens; no matter what your speed, the speed of light is always the same.

After much thought, Einstein showed that the only way that the speed of light could always be the same was if distances shrink and clocks slow down at high speeds. In normal life, we never travel fast enough to notice these strange effects.

But, imagine that the speed of light was only 10 mph; then a friend cycling along the street would be traveling near the speed of light. If you were able to compare your friend's watch with your own watch as he or she cycled by, you would see that the other watch was slower than yours.

Also, from your position, the cyclist would appear to be shrunken or compressed lengthways. The cyclist would not notice a change in his or her size. Instead, the buildings at the side of the street would appear thin and compressed. This shrinking effect is called the Fitzgerald-Lorentz contraction, after the Irish physicist George Fitzgerald, who first suggested it, and the Dutch physicist Hendrick A. Lorentz. Here is another limerick:

> There was a young fellow named Fisk
> Whose fencing was exceedingly brisk;
> So fast was his action,
> The Fitzgerald contraction
> Reduced his sword to a disk.

A strange effect of high speed. A cyclist traveling at near the speed of light would appear contracted when viewed by a stationary onlooker. At the same time, the cyclist would notice that the houses and any onlookers would appear contracted. This effect, called the Fitzgerald-Lorentz contraction, was explained by Einstein.

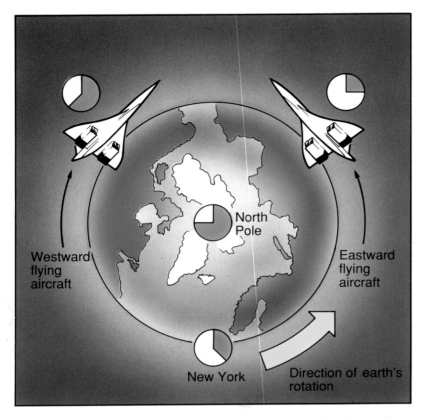

North Pole

Westward flying aircraft

Eastward flying aircraft

New York

Direction of earth's rotation

Clocks on board airplanes show that Einstein's ideas about the effect of speed on time are correct. Imagine that two ultra-accurate atomic clocks have been synchronized against a clock in New York. Then one clock is flown eastward around the world (in the direction of the earth's rotation), and the other clock is flown westward. When the clocks return to New York, it is seen that the eastward-flying clock was running slow during the flight and has lost time compared with the stationary clock in New York. The westward-flying clock runs fast during the flight and gains time. Because of the earth's rotation, the clock at New York is moving relative to a clock at the North Pole, so it runs slow.

The rhyme suggests that Mr. Fisk could thrust his sword forward at nearly the speed of light. To watching spectators, his sword would appear shortened. The rhyme is slightly inaccurate because the sword would not appear as a disk.

Strange as they may seem, Einstein's ideas have been proved correct by many experiments. For example, in 1971, very sensitive clocks – called

Stretching time

In 1978, scientists at the CERN laboratories in Geneva, Switzerland (below), accelerated minute particles, called muons, to nearly the speed of light. The life of these particles is extremely short – they normally explode after about two-millionths of a second. But, in the CERN experiment, the muons' life was extended by twenty times because, at their great speed, time was slowed down by twenty times. Careful measurements showed that their extended life was exactly as predicted by Einstein's theory of special relativity.

atomic clocks – were carried around the world in high-speed aircraft and then compared with identical clocks left on the ground. The clocks that had traveled at high speed were found to have slowed down by 0.0000001 second; this small effect showed that time had slowed down on the moving aircraft.

4 ▽ A Famous Professor

Robert Brown (1773–1858), the Scottish scientist who, in 1827, first observed that tiny particles of dust on water are constantly in motion, as if alive. No one could explain the observation, and some people thought the particles were displaying a new form of life.

Einstein's work on relativity was published in 1905. In the same year he published another important work about the behavior of molecules and atoms, which are very small particles. In those days, some scientists were not completely convinced that atoms and molecules really existed, but Einstein proved that they did. He showed that molecules in a liquid would bump into very small dust particles on the liquid surface, making the dust particles jump as if they were alive. These jumping movements, called Brownian movements, had been observed by a Scottish scientist, Robert Brown, in 1827 but, until Einstein, no one had been able to explain what caused them.

In 1905, Einstein also published his ideas about light. Light, Einstein said, was made up of particles, which he called photons. A beam of light is like a stream of photons. Using this idea, he was able to explain the "photoelectric effect" – the production of electricity by light. He showed that when light shines onto the surface of a metal, electrons – particles of electricity – are knocked out of the metal atoms by the photons, producing an electric current.

Experiments by other scientists showed that Einstein's ideas about light must be correct but, nevertheless, a puzzle remained. There was a lot of evidence that showed that light was made up of waves, called electromagnetic waves. How could light be both a particle and a wave at the same time? This was a question that was to puzzle Einstein all his life.

In 1905, Albert Einstein explained Brown's observations. The particles were jumping because they were being buffeted by water molecules. Because molecules move more rapidly at higher temperatures, the particle movements are greater.

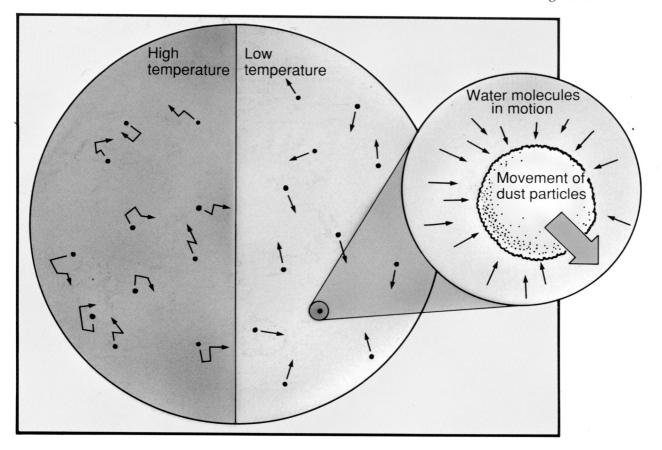

High temperature

Low temperature

Water molecules in motion

Movement of dust particles

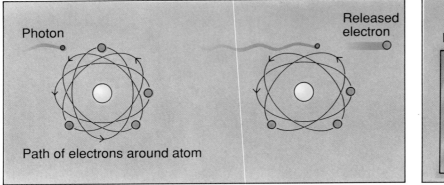

Photon

Path of electrons around atom

Released electron

Metal plate

Electrons

In 1908, Einstein began teaching part-time, at the University of Bern. The following year, when he was thirty, he became a full-time teacher at Zurich University. His lectures were not very popular – sometimes as few as two pupils attended. On one occasion, Einstein was scolded by a senior professor because his lectures were so dull. Einstein replied that he could always fall back on his "shoemaker's job" if he was dismissed.

In 1911, Einstein was offered a professorship at the University of Prague (in present-day Czechoslovakia). His mother's prediction that he would be a professor had come true! The Einsteins – Albert, Mileva, and their two sons, Hans Albert and Eduard – moved to Prague, but they were only there for a year and a half. By now, Einstein's reputation was worldwide, and many universities were eager to have him on their staff.

In 1912, he moved to Zurich Polytechnic, where at the age of sixteen he had failed the entrance examination. Then, in the spring of 1914, he moved to the University of Berlin, the capital of Germany, where he became research director at the important new Institute of Physics. At the time, it was said that only twelve people understood Einstein's work, and eight of them lived in Berlin. This was not true, but Einstein must have looked forward to working with other world-famous scientists at the Institute.

Above The photoelectric effect: when light falls on some metals, electricity in the form of electrons "shoots" from the metal. Einstein explained that particles of light – called photons – were knocking the electrons out of the metal atoms.

Opposite The photoelectric effect is used in this particle detector at the CERN laboratory, Switzerland. Particles passing through the large sheet of acrylic plastic at the top produce light. This light is converted into an electrical signal by the photomultiplier at the bottom, using the photoelectric effect.

Einstein was, in many ways, the very picture of an absent-minded professor, always engrossed in his calculations. Even on the day he and Mileva were married, his thoughts were

A painting showing the horrors of World War I. Einstein was a pacifist all his life. He was convinced that war was the greatest evil of all and that scientists should not allow their inventions to be used for destruction.

elsewhere. When the couple arrived at their lodgings late at night after the wedding, Einstein found that he had forgotten his door key. The landlord had to be awakened to let them in. Later in life, Einstein sometimes forgot his own address while out walking and had to telephone the university for directions back to his house.

Einstein did not give much thought to his appearance. He disliked wearing socks, gave his lectures in shabby clothes, and wore trousers that were too short. His lack of interest in clothes lasted all his life. Many years later, Einstein called on a teacher who had encouraged him when he was young. However, he seemed to his old teacher to be only a beggar in shabby clothes, and the visit ended promptly.

In August 1914, World War I began. For safety, Mileva and the boys moved back to Zurich. Unhappily, the Einsteins' marriage was almost over. Both Albert and Mileva realized that they were not suited to each other, although they did not divorce until 1919.

Einstein (middle) with his second wife, Elsa, and Richard Haldane in London in 1921. Haldane was a British politician who was Secretary for War just before World War I. No doubt Einstein expressed his disapproval of war to Haldane.

Einstein was a pacifist who did not believe in war as a way of settling disputes between nations. He was horrified by the use of new weapons, such as poison gas, invented by scientists. To him this was a misuse of science. He thought that Germany was to blame for the war, and he helped to write an article calling for peace and international cooperation. Einstein also helped to form a political party that sought to end the war; however, the party was outlawed by the German government in 1916.

Einstein's great interest at this time was to complete his theory of gravity, which he had begun in 1907. In 1916, he published a paper called *The General Theory of Relativity*, which outlined his latest idea.

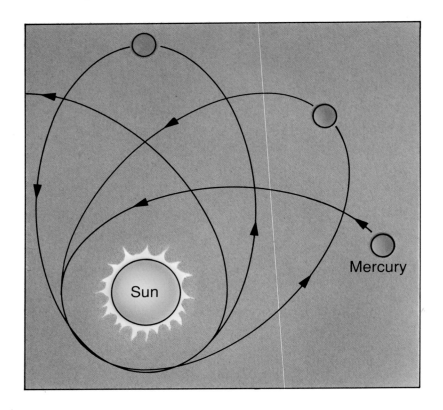

Most planets go around the sun in a nearly circular path. However, the planet nearest the sun, Mercury, goes around in a rosette-shaped path. Einstein, using his theory of gravity, was the first to explain why this happens.

Gravity is one of the most important forces of all. It is the force that draws any two objects together. The force of gravity makes objects fall when we drop them; it is gravity that keeps you in your seat when you sit down. On a larger scale, it is the force of gravity that keeps the moon circling around the earth, and the planets circling around the sun.

Einstein set out to explain what caused gravity. He called the space between two objects, where the force of gravity was evident, a gravitational "field." He soon discovered that the gravitational field is like a stretched rubber sheet. When a heavy object is placed on the sheet, the sheet is indented. Place a small object, such as a marble, on the sheet as well, and it will roll toward the heavy object.

Gravity and time

A strange prediction made by Einstein was that clocks should run slower where the force of gravity is strong. Just as fast motion slows time down, so does strong gravity. In 1963, this prediction was tested using ultra-accurate atomic clocks. Clocks at the top of a tall tower were compared with clocks at the bottom of the tower, where gravity is slightly stronger. The effect was confirmed: the clocks at the bottom ran slightly slower than those at the top. Then, in 1976, a rocket carried an atomic clock into space, where gravity is weaker. The clock was found to run one-millionth of a second faster in space, proving that Einstein was correct.

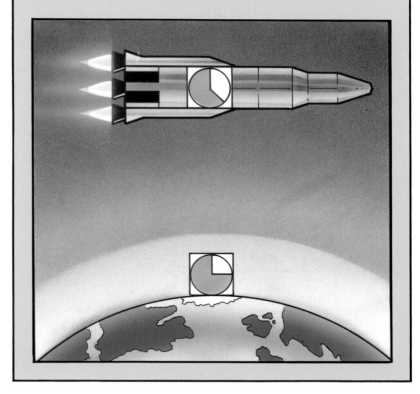

Of course, Einstein was not saying that there really is a rubber sheet stretching through the space between objects. However, his mathematical calculations showed him that there was something called "space-time" which acted in

Black holes

One of the dramatic predictions of general relativity was the "black hole," caused by a small object with immense gravity. A black hole forms when a very large star shrinks under the force of its own gravity. It is as if a very small, but very heavy, ball were placed on the "rubber sheet" of space-time making a deep, well-like dent in the sheet, from which nothing can escape.

If you should fall into a black hole, you would never get out again! As you fell into the hole feet first, the gravity at your feet would be millions of times stronger than at your head and, as a result, your body would be stretched out like a thin piece of wire hundreds of miles long.

In the intense gravity field around a black hole, time slows down. Events near the hole – seen from a safe distance – would seem to be happening at a snail's pace. Inside the hole, time stops completely. A light beam trying to escape from the hole would appear trapped – frozen in time – which is why the hole seems black.

An artist's impression of a black hole (center) being circled by an orange-red star (upper right). Gas is being pulled from the atmosphere of the star by the immense gravitational field of the black hole. As the gas spirals down into the black hole, it forms a flat disk that heats up (white region) and gives out x-rays. The picture shows the star system as seen from the rocky surface of a planet, which is being drawn into the black hole.

According to Einstein, gravity affects light. A light beam from a distant star that passes close to a massive object is bent by the curvature of "space-time." The star's position appears to have shifted.

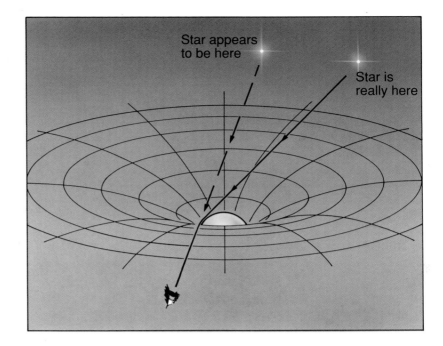

a very similar way to the rubber sheet. Space-time is a combination of space and time. It is hard to visualize space-time, and Einstein had to use complicated mathematics to describe it.

Einstein knew that other scientists would not believe his theory unless he could make predictions about gravity that other scientists could test. His first prediction was that light should be affected by gravity. When a beam of light traveled across the "rubber sheet" of space-time, its path should bend near a heavy object because of the "dent" in space-time caused by the object.

In 1919, there was an opportunity to test this prediction. In that year, an eclipse of the sun occurred and, during the few minutes of darkness, it was possible to measure the position of stars in the direction of the sun to see if light from them was affected by the gravity of the sun. A British astronomer named Arthur Eddington led an expedition of astronomers to the island of Principe, off the coast of West Africa, to observe the eclipse. Another expedition of astronomers observed the eclipse from Sobral in Brazil.

Right *Arthur Eddington (1882–1946) was an English astronomer. He led an expedition to West Africa to see if starlight was affected in the way that Einstein said. He later wrote several books on Einstein's theories.*

Below *A solar eclipse of June 11, 1983, during which the moon passed in front of the sun. By observing the stars near the sun during such an eclipse, astronomers proved that gravity affects light.*

Both expeditions found that the light from the stars was affected just as Einstein had predicted. When the news reached Europe, Einstein became famous overnight. "Light caught bending!" screamed large newspaper headlines. Relativity became the talk of Europe and the United States. Newspapers scrambled for writers who could explain it simply. One offered a prize for an article of 3,000 words – jokingly, Einstein said the competition was too hard even for him to enter!

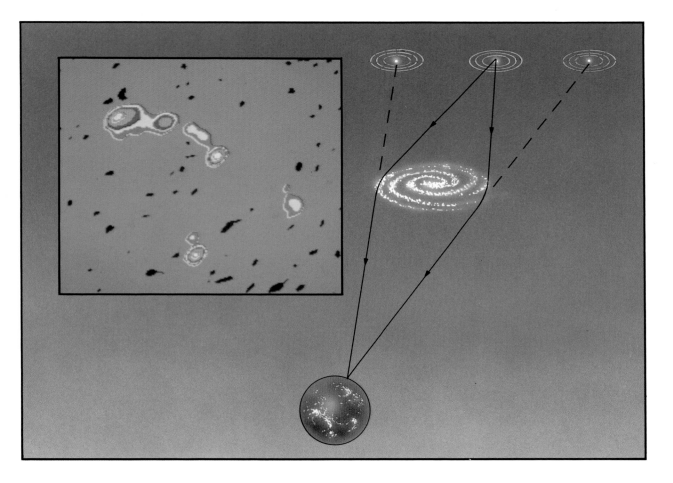

*A computer-colored picture (**inset**) of a distant star system called a quasar. The quasar is a single object, but we see two images of it (the blue circles one above the other at the center of the picture). This is because the light from it is bent when it passes close to a collection of stars (the small yellow and red patch just above the bottom image of the quasar), which acts as a "gravitational lens." The discovery of the double image in 1979 confirms Einstein's theory of gravity.*

6   "God Does Not Play Dice"

The end of World War I in 1918 brought many changes to Einstein's life. On a personal level, he divorced Mileva, and married his cousin, Elsa Lowenthal. Also, his Jewish roots became increasingly important to him. Since living in Prague, before the war, he had been aware of anti-semitism (anti-Jewish) feelings. Now in Germany, Einstein increasingly became the target of anti-semitic prejudice.

Anti-semitism in Germany during the Nazi era. An illustration from a children's book of the time shows children reading an anti-Jewish newspaper. Sinister-looking "Jewish" figures hover nearby.

Einstein (center) arriving in
the United States in 1921,
with his wife (on his left).
With the Einsteins are
leading Zionists.

Some German scientists called his theories
"Jewish physics" and tried to discredit them.
Einstein attended one of their public meetings and
showed great amusement at their errors and
distortions. But although the arguments against
his ideas were feeble and could not succeed, the
situation was serious. In 1921, a young Berliner
was convicted of offering a reward for Einstein's
murder. As a pacifist and a Jew, Einstein was to
live with the threat of assassination for some time.

In the spring and early summer of 1921,
Einstein visited the United States and Britain. He
made fund-raising speeches, arguing for a Jewish
homeland in Palestine. He also gave lectures
about his theories, for there was great public
interest in his ideas.

Wave or particle?

Is light made up of waves or particles? Einstein showed how the photoelectric effect could be explained if light is made up of point-like particles called photons. However, there are many situations where one beam of light cancels out another beam, producing a pattern of bright and dark bands (see below). This could only happen if light were made up of waves – dark bands form where the crest of one wave is canceled out by the trough of the other wave. So, is light made of spread-out waves or point-like particles?

Quantum theory sorts out the problem by saying that a light beam is made of both waves and particles. We cannot say exactly where the particles are at any one time, but the waves show where they are most likely to be found. According to quantum theory, electrons are also both waves and particles at the same time.

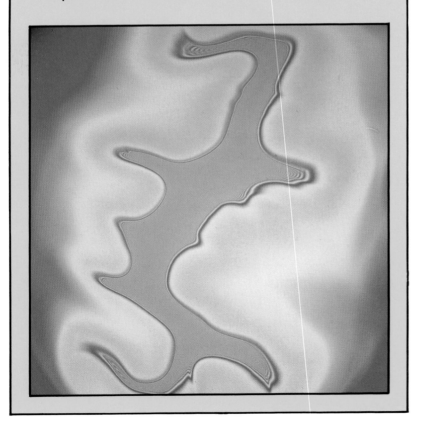

A pioneer of quantum theory, Max Born (right), in Stockholm in 1954 to receive the Nobel Prize for Physics. Born helped to show that events inside atoms happen almost by chance. With Born is the British ambassador to Sweden.

In his lectures, Einstein stressed the need to renew scientific and cultural links across Europe. He was appalled by the horrors and destruction of war, and he believed that a non-competitive, non-patriotic form of education was the key to a peaceful world. He argued that the world should turn to socialism and governments should share out the wealth of the world in a fair way.

In 1922, Einstein was awarded the Nobel Prize for Physics. The Nobel Prize is given each year to a scientist who has made an important discovery. Einstein's prize was for his explanation of the photoelectric effect, although some people considered this as only a small part of his work. He gave all the prize money to Mileva, his former wife.

Toward the end of the 1920s, he was beginning to lose his place at the forefront of scientific thought. He was unhappy about the new ideas being developed about the behavior of atoms. These ideas, called quantum theory, suggested that events inside atoms occur almost by chance.

Niels Bohr, a Danish physicist who developed a new theory of the atom, based on new quantum ideas that Einstein could not accept. Bohr and Einstein argued for thirty years over the new ideas. In this field, Einstein was out of step with the rest of the scientific world.

Einstein could not accept this. In 1926, he wrote to the German physicist Max Born: "Quantum theory accomplishes a lot, but it does not bring us close to the secrets of the Old One. In any case, I am convinced that He does not play dice."

Einstein called the new theories "a gentle pillow from which the believer is not easily roused." As one might imagine, he was not inclined to let the "true believers" – who included most of the world's leading scientists – sleep in peace. For thirty years, he argued against the quantum theory. His particular opponent, the Danish physicist Niels Bohr, had helped to develop the new theory. In 1930, at a conference in Brussels, Belgium, Einstein thought that he had settled the argument. He invented a theoretical device involving clocks and measuring scales that appeared to show that quantum theory was wrong. After a sleepless night, Bohr discovered that in his reasoning, Einstein had forgotten to take into account his own discovery that clocks run at a slower rate in a gravitational field. When this was taken into account, Einstein had no answer, and the new theory triumphed.

All these arguments were conducted with good humor. Anyone who talked to Einstein was impressed by his simple, lovable character. He was never angry or impatient, and he never tried to make his opponent look foolish. He was only interested in finding the truth. And, if he made mistakes, he was ready to admit it. His papers are full of such phrases as, "Four years ago, I tried to answer the question whether light is affected by gravity. I return to this question now because my previous ideas now do not satisfy me."

On quantum theory, however, Einstein would not admit defeat. He remained convinced that the theory was wrong, despite the great number of accurate predictions made by the theory. Quantum theory has turned out to be one of the most successful theories of all time, which goes to show that even scientists as great as Einstein can sometimes be wrong.

Albert Einstein with his daughter and her husband on a sailing vacation in 1930. Sailing was one of Einstein's greatest pleasures.

Einstein's fiftieth birthday, in 1929, brought many honors and messages of congratulations from around the world. Over the next few years, he made several trips to the United States and Britain, and he continued his campaign for world peace. He called for the world's workers to stop producing guns and ammunition, and to refuse to serve in their countries' armies. This, he said, would prevent future wars.

Adolf Hitler touring the streets of Nazi Germany in 1934. The Nazis were known as "brownshirts" because of their brown uniforms.

In 1933, while Einstein was in the United States, Adolf Hitler became Chancellor of Germany. Anti-semitic hysteria rose to fever pitch and, once again, Einstein's theories were attacked as "Jewish physics." Along with the writings of many other Jews, pacifists and anti-Nazis, his books were burned publicly. His home was broken into, and his belongings taken or destroyed. His portrait was published in a book of "national enemies," and underneath the picture were the words: "Not yet hanged." To return to Germany now was completely out of the question.

Einstein stayed for a few months in Belgium, and then moved to a village on the coast of Norfolk, in England. Here he was guarded by two young women with shotguns; there was a rumor that the Nazis had a large reward equivalent to thousands of dollars on his head. Wryly, he said he hardly knew it was worth so much.

Einstein and Ernest Rutherford at a meeting in London in 1933 to discuss how refugees from Nazi Germany could be helped. Rutherford was a famous New Zealand scientist who discovered the atomic nucleus in 1911.

At the end of 1933, Einstein and his wife, Elsa, emigrated to the United States, where they were made welcome. Within a few weeks, they were invited to dine and stay overnight with President Franklin D. Roosevelt in the White House. Einstein took up an appointment at Princeton University where he continued his search for a theory, called a "unified theory," to explain electrical and magnetic forces as well as gravity.

In December 1936, Einstein's wife died. He continued his frugal and simple life, and maintained his efforts to help Jewish scientists who were in danger from the Nazis. He gave violin recitals in New York, raising over $6,000 to help persecuted scientists.

In 1939, four weeks before Hitler started World War II by invading Poland, Einstein wrote a now famous letter to President Roosevelt

telling of the possibility of a new kind of bomb –
the atomic bomb – and warning the President that
the Nazis might develop the new bomb first.

Einstein did not invent the atomic bomb, but he
did state the principle on which the bomb is based:
$E = mc^2$ or, to put it another way, enormous
energy can be released by converting matter into
energy. President Roosevelt understood the
importance of Einstein's letter and, when the
United States entered the war in 1942, he set a
team of scientists to work to make the atomic

$E = mc^2$

Perhaps the most dramatic of Einstein's theories
was that solid objects can be converted into pure
energy. This is what happens inside a nuclear
reactor or when a nuclear bomb explodes (below).
Einstein summed up this idea in a famous formula
$E = mc^2$. In this formula, E represents the energy
of an object, m is the mass of the object, and c is the
speed of light. Because the speed of light is so
great, c is a large number. The formula shows that
a small amount of mass can be converted into a
large amount of energy. A mere 0.000002 lb
(0.000001 kg) of matter, converted into energy,
would be enough to send a rocket into space.

bomb. Einstein was not officially involved, but he knew of the team's existence. When the first bombs were ready for use, he sent another letter to the President, this time urging that the bombs should not be used. Despite his plea, two atomic bombs were dropped on Japan in August 1945. More than 100,000 people were killed instantly, and many more died from the aftereffects.

For the rest of his life, Einstein called for the abolition of nuclear weapons. "The war is won, but the peace is not," he declared. In broadcasts, speeches and interviews, he called for international cooperation and a world government. He believed that the world was on the brink of complete destruction by nuclear

On August 6, 1945, toward the end of World War II, a single atomic bomb was dropped on the Japanese city of Hiroshima, killing at least 137,000 people out of a population of 343,000.

warfare. "Science has brought forth this danger," he wrote, "but the real problem is in the hearts and minds of men."

In 1952, Einstein was asked if he would become President of the State of Israel, which had been formed in 1948 in Palestine. Einstein, deeply moved, turned the offer down. He pointed out, in a typically humble way, that he lacked the experience to deal properly with diplomats and important politicians. He hated formal occasions, especially the need to wear formal clothes. When he was called upon to make an after-dinner speech, he did his best to please – but, privately, he called these affairs "feeding times at the zoo."

As for his scientific research, he continued it until the day of his death – April 18, 1955. At his hospital bedside was a paper with his latest calculations. His search for a unified theory of all forces proved unsuccessful, but other scientists would take up the task he left uncompleted.

David Ben-Gurion proclaiming the birth of the new state of Israel on May 24, 1948.

Einstein was one of the greatest scientists of all time. The only other physicist who was as important was the Englishman Isaac Newton, who lived from 1642 to 1727. There are interesting similarities between the work of Newton and Einstein. Both investigated space and time, and the way that forces cause objects to move. To Newton, space was a kind of unvarying "framework" within which we live. Time was like a "river" that flowed along at the same pace whatever we might do, or whoever might measure it. In other words, Newton believed in "absolute" space and time. These ideas were believed by most scientists for over two hundred years until Einstein showed that they were wrong. Space and time are "relative"; measurements of time and space can be different when different people do the measuring, and there is no point in asking which measurement is "correct."

Both Newton and Einstein put forward theories about gravity. Newton's theory of gravity was the first explanation of the earth's path around the sun. This theory is still used for tasks such as calculating the paths of spacecraft as they fly through space. However, Einstein's theory of gravity is used now where gravity is very strong,

Einstein and his daughter take the oath of citizenship in the United States in 1940.

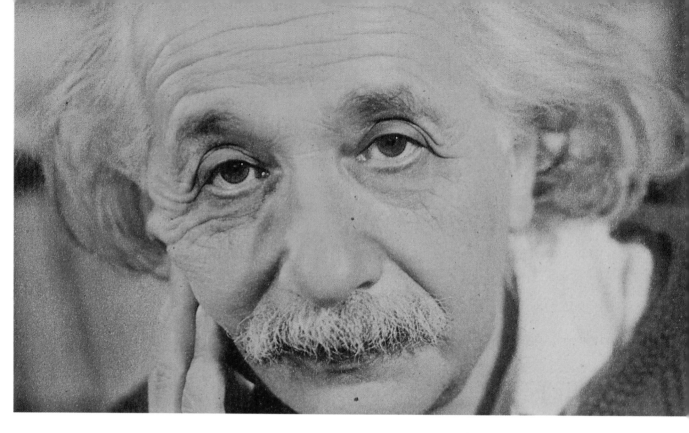

Albert Einstein was one of the greatest scientists of all time. He died in 1955 at the age of 76.

for example, near a black hole.

Almost single-handedly, Einstein began modern physics. His explanation of the photoelectric effect spurred on other scientists to develop quantum theory. His ideas about space, time and gravity were revolutionary. Working out the consequences of these ideas, Einstein made amazing discoveries: light beams could be bent by gravity, and matter could be converted into energy. As a result of his far-reaching discoveries, a terrible new weapon – the atomic bomb – came into being.

Einstein was quick to point out the dangers of the new weapon. To his great credit, Einstein was not content to let politicians, army generals and businessmen decide how the discoveries of science should be used. We all must play our part, he said. Today, as we see the effects of pollution and the dangers of global warming, we should remember Einstein's advice.

Date Chart

1879 March 14: Albert Einstein born in Ulm, a town in southern Germany.

1884 Albert's encounter with a compass.

1894 Albert joins his parents and sister in Milan, Italy.

1895–6 Fails entrance exam for Zurich Polytechnic.

1896 Enters Zurich Polytechnic after taking entrance exam again; renounces German citizenship.

1896–1900 Studies to become a teacher.

1901 Takes Swiss nationality; publishes his first scientific paper.

1902 Starts work at the Patent Office in Bern.

1903 Marries Mileva Maric.

1905 Writes his first important scientific papers, including two on *The Special Theory of Relativity*; one about the behavior of light particles; and two about Brownian movement.

1908 Receives doctor's degree from the University of Bern.

1909 Becomes junior professor at Zurich Polytechnic.

1911 Becomes professor at University of Prague.

1912 Returns to Zurich as professor of physics.

1914 Moves to Berlin as research director at the Institute of Physics; start of World War I.

1916 Publishes the *The General Theory of Relativity*.

1918 End of World War I.

1919 Divorces Mileva and marries Elsa Lowenthal. Eclipse observations confirm theory of general relativity.

1921 Lecture tours to U.S. and Britain.

1922 Awarded Nobel Prize for his work on photoelectric effect.

1924–30 Continuing peace work; connections with the League of Nations. Begins work on a unified theory.

1930–3 Further visits to U.S. and Britain.

1933 Hitler becomes leader of Germany. Einstein takes temporary refuge in Belgium and Britain, then moves permanently to the United States, to Princeton University.

1939 Start of World War II; letter to President Roosevelt suggesting atomic bomb research.

1941 Takes U.S. citizenship.

1945 Atomic bombs dropped on Japanese cities of Hiroshima and Nagasaki end World War II; Einstein retires from Princeton.

1946 Begins campaign against nuclear weapons.

1952 Turns down offer to become President of Israel.

1955 Dies on April 18 at Princeton.

Glossary

Atom A very small particle of matter. Everything is made up of atoms.

Black hole A region in space with gravity so strong that light cannot escape.

Brownian movements Small, jumping movements made by dust particles floating on a liquid.

Electromagnetic waves A ripple of electricity and magnetism that travels through space. Radio waves, microwaves, x-rays and light are electromagnetic waves.

Electron A particle of electricity. An electric current is a stream of electrons.

Energy The capacity to do work, such as lifting objects.

Geometry A branch of mathematics that deals with points, lines and shapes.

Gravitational field The area of space around an object where the effects of the force of gravity can be seen.

Gravitational Lens An arrangement of objects in space that focuses the light from distant galaxies by using the gravity of objects lying between the earth and the galaxies.

Mass The amount of matter in an object. Mass is different from weight because weight depends on gravity, but mass is always the same.

Molecule A small particle made up of atoms joined together.

Nobel Prize A prize given each year to a person who has made an important discovery.

Orbit The path that a planet takes while circling the sun or that a satellite follows as it circles a planet.

Photoelectric effect The way some electrons are released from some metals when light falls on the metal.

Photon A particle of light. A beam of light is a stream of photons.

Physicist A person who studies physics, the science of matter, energy and forces.

Quantum theory The theory that describes the behavior of very small objects, such as atoms and electrons.

Relativity Einstein's theory of high speeds and gravity.

Socialism A political system aimed at establishing a fair society in which the government owns all land, buildings and businesses.

Space-time A combination of space and time.

Special relativity Einstein's theory that describes how objects behave when moving at very high speeds, near the speed of light.

Books to Read

Dank, Milton. *Albert Einstein*. New York: Franklin Watts, 1983.

Farr, Naunerle. *Madame Curie – Albert Einstein*. Westhaven, CT: Pendulum Press, 1979.

Hunter, Nigel. *Einstein*. New York: Franklin Watts, 1987.

Ireland, Karin. *Albert Einstein*. Englewood Cliffs, NJ: Silver Burdett Press, 1989.

Index

Picture Acknowledgments

Mary Evans 14, 20, 36, 38; Mansell Collection *cover*, iii, 6, 7, 8; Popperfoto 30, 35, 40, 42, 43; Science Photo Library 19, 23, 28, 30, 31 (inset), 34; Topham 5, 24, 32, 41, 44, 45; Wayland Picture Library 9, 10, 11, 12, 13, 15, 25, 33, 37, 39. Illustrations by Brian Davey. Cover artwork by Richard Hook.

DATE DUE
